FORENSIC PSYCHOLOGIST

SUSAN H. GRAY

Published in the United States of America by Cherry Lake Publishing
Ann Arbor, Michigan
www.cherrylakepublishing.com

Content Adviser: Jeffrey M. Jentzen, M.D., Ph.D., Professor, Department of Pathology, and Director,
Autopsy and Forensic Services at the University of Michigan Health System
Reading Adviser: Marla Conn, ReadAbility, Inc.

Photo Credits: © Stockbyte/Thinkstock Images, cover, 1, 25, 29; © Dariush M/Shutterstock.com, 5; © Olimpik/
Shutterstock Images, 6; © fstop/iStock.com, 9; © Fuse/Thinkstock Images, 10; © Andrey Burmakin/Shutterstock
Images, 12; © TFoxFoto/Shutterstock.com, 15; © Image Point Fr/Shutterstock Images, 16; © bikeriderlondon/
Shutterstock Images, 17, 18; © tab62/Shutterstock Images, 21; © John Gomez/Shutterstock Images, 22; © Monkey
Business Images, 27

Library of Congress Cataloging-in-Publication Data

Gray, Susan H.
  Forensic psychologist/Susan H. Gray.
    pages cm.—(Cool STEAM careers)
  Audience: Age 8–12.
  Audience: Grade 4 to 6.
  Includes index.
  ISBN 978-1-63362-559-4 (hardcover)—ISBN 978-1-63362-649-2 (pbk.)—ISBN 978-1-63362-739-0 (pdf)—
ISBN 978-1-63362-829-8 (ebook)
  1. Forensic psychology—Juvenile literature. I. Title.

RA1148.G74 2016
614'.15—dc23
                            2015005360

Cherry Lake Publishing would like to acknowledge the work of
the Partnership for 21st Century Skills. Please visit www.p21.org
for more information.

Printed in the United States of America
Corporate Graphics

ABOUT THE AUTHOR

Susan H. Gray has a master's degree in zoology and has written many reference books for children
and young adults. In her free time, she enjoys traveling, gardening, and playing the piano. Susan
and her husband, Michael, live in Cabot, Arkansas, with their many pets.

TABLE OF CONTENTS

STEAM is the acronym for Science, Technology, Engineering, Arts, and Mathematics. In this book, you will read about how each of these study areas is connected to a career in forensic psychology.

CHAPTER 1

Psychology Meets the Law

Ming was watching television with her mother. Suddenly, the show was interrupted by a news flash. A restaurant downtown was on fire. This was the town's third major fire in a month. The newscaster stated that the police suspected it was **arson**, or a fire set on purpose. "That's awful. Why would anyone do that?" Ming asked, shocked.

Her mother sighed. "That's for a **forensic** psychologist to figure out," she said. "That's a psychologist who has special training that can be used in legal cases." She added,

"A psychologist studies how people behave and how their minds work. A forensic scientist uses science to solve legal questions, often about crimes. Forensic psychologists are experts who pull together their knowledge of both fields."

In a way, forensic psychologists are like detectives. To arrive at the facts, they ask all kinds of questions related to mental and legal issues. Does the person know the

Forensic psychologists are sometimes called in to look at arson cases.

Some forensic psychologists talk to children who have witnessed crimes.

difference between right and wrong? Is the person well enough to take part in a trial? Is he or she mentally ill, or just pretending to be? Questions like these help determine the amount of responsibility on the **defendant**. It is important for forensic psychologists to present their findings clearly and accurately. Their expert opinions can greatly influence the outcome of the cases they work on.

Criminal behavior is not the only focus of forensic psychologists. They can help lawyers select jury members. They can analyze the testimony of **witnesses**.

They might work with small children who are afraid to appear in court. Outside the courts, forensic psychologists often interview those who want to work as police officers, to see if they are stable, rational people.

Forensic psychologists also assist in divorce cases, helping to determine which parent the children will live with. Or they might interview elderly people to see if they are able to make decisions about their medical care. As psychologists, they want to understand the people they work with. As forensic psychologists, they apply their understanding to situations that involve the law.

THINK ABOUT TECHNOLOGY

Suppose a forensic psychologist wonders if there's an unusually high rate of a particular inherited disease in the prison population. To find out, the researcher must gather and analyze large amounts of data. Such a study would require the use of computers and specialized software.

CHAPTER 2

A Developing Field

Forensic psychology has changed considerably over the years. Before the 1880s, psychologists were not allowed to lend their **expertise** to legal cases at all. Outcomes often depended largely on **eyewitness** testimonies. But in 1893, James Cattell at Columbia University began to research the psychology of testimony. He gathered 56 college students and asked each of them the same set of questions. For example, students had to tell him what the weather was like a week earlier. Cattell also asked the students to rate their level of confidence in their answers.

As it turned out, many students gave wrong answers but were highly confident that they were correct. Other students answered correctly but were unsure of their answers. Regarding the weather question, students gave answers all across the range of possibilities. Cattell's experiment showed how unreliable people's memories could be.

Sometimes witnesses think that they saw things that didn't really happen.

Witnesses who speak in trials need to take vows that they will tell the truth.

The first recorded instance of a psychologist taking part in a trial was in 1896. A man in Germany was accused of three murders. As the trial approached, stories about the crimes were splashed across newspapers. The stories were full of details and reports from various people. At the trial, many witnesses said they saw the murders and described what they saw. Then psychologist Albert von Schrenck-Notzing was called as an **expert witness**. He had done research on how memory works. He said the witnesses couldn't tell the difference between what they really saw and what they had read in the newspapers.

Psychologist William Stern began studying memory in 1901. He found that certain kinds of questions could produce false memories. For example, he might ask, "Did you see the man with the knife?" That's called a "leading question" because it leads the person toward a specific answer. The person might say yes, even if the man had no knife. Stern's studies shed more light on eyewitness reports.

THINK ABOUT MATH

The best forensic psychologists understand how good research is conducted. They also have a grasp of the mathematical science of statistics. They can read a research paper and tell whether the researcher was sloppy or had a well-designed experiment. Their knowledge of statistics can help them understand the conclusions drawn by the researcher.

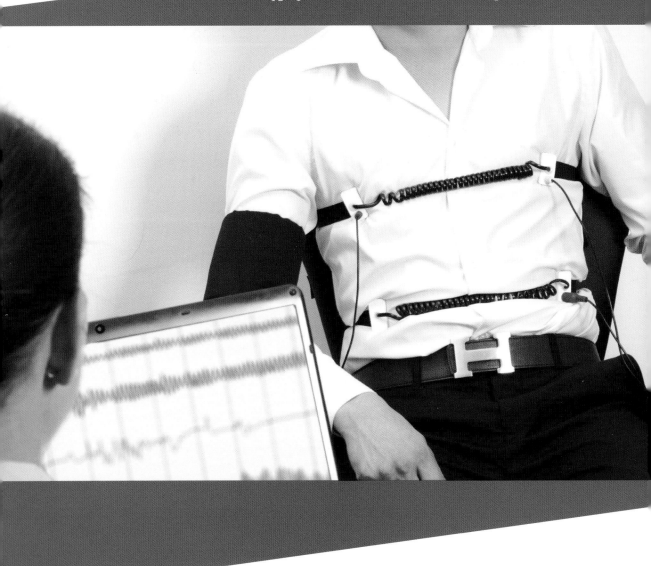

Polygraphs, or lie detectors, are not always accurate.

About 20 years later, psychologist William Marston suggested that when people are lying, their blood pressure rises. This led to the invention of the modern polygraph, or lie detector. Polygraph test results cannot be used in most courts. People have questioned their reliability throughout the device's history. Today, experts realize that many factors can affect the test's results. Psychologists disagree about whether polygraphs are reliable. But they are still sometimes used in police investigations.

For years, medical doctors were considered better expert witnesses than psychologists. In 1940, courts ruled that expert witnesses must have a lot of knowledge about the subject they testify on. Medical doctors aren't always experts in psychology. So gradually, psychologists gained acceptance in the legal system.

CHAPTER 3

WORKING AS A FORENSIC PSYCHOLOGIST

In recent years, many crime dramas have presented forensic psychologists as leading exciting lives. They solve crimes. They have special **insight** into how criminals think. They use equipment and computer programs to spot clues that everyone else has missed. Unfortunately, this is not an accurate picture of the work these psychologists do.

Most work falls into either civil law or criminal law. Civil law includes legal cases involving personal injury suits, workers' compensation, and child **custody**.

Forensic psychologists sometimes talk to car accident victims to help figure out what really happened.

Suppose a woman is injured in a car accident. This is a personal injury situation. She claims she has suffered chronic pain as a result of the accident. She wants lots of money from the guilty driver because of her injury. A forensic psychologist would question the woman to see if her claims are true.

For a workers' compensation suit, the forensic psychologist might interview a worker who claims to have been injured on the job. The psychologist might also talk to doctors who are familiar with such injuries.

Sometimes, when parents get divorced, a forensic psychologist will help decide which parent is better for the child to live with.

He or she tries to determine whether the worker is faking or **exaggerating** the injury, or has a **legitimate** claim.

In child custody cases, the psychologist will separately interview the parents and children involved. The psychologist wants to ensure that the children are at ease during their interviews. It is important that everyone feels free to speak honestly about their feelings. After the interviews—and maybe even some visits to the home—the forensic psychologist will make custody recommendations to the judge.

Criminal cases might involve the psychologist meeting with accused individuals, victims, police officers, and even prison administrators. In an interview, the accused might be asked to explain what happened before, during, and after the crime. They are asked why they did it and what they were thinking and feeling at the time. Other questions may cover the person's childhood, family and friends, jobs, drug and alcohol abuse, physical

A judge might listen to what a forensic psychologist has discovered about an accused criminal.

Some forensic psychologists teach at universities.

abuse, or medical problems. Throughout this process, the forensic psychologist listens for possible lies.

If people are found guilty and will be **incarcerated**, the psychologist could very well meet with their prison administrators. Here, the psychologist could suggest counseling programs or prison jobs that might benefit the criminals or help them turn their lives around.

Forensic psychologists have a range of other job options, too. Many teach in universities. Some have private practices where they focus on helping crime victims. Others do research in forensic sciences. Still others interview applicants for jobs in law enforcement. Today, thousands of people serve as forensic psychologists. Their jobs are often stressful and, in extreme cases, dangerous. But being a forensic psychologist can be very satisfying.

THINK ABOUT ENGINEERING

Forensic psychologists often consult with experts in other fields. In their daily work, they might have to speak with doctors, scientists, teachers, or engineers. Engineers, for example, can help with workers' compensation suits. They can explain how a factory's poor design led to a worker's injury. Or they might explain how a worker ignored safety rules before being injured.

SOME CURRENT TOPICS

The field of forensic psychology is constantly changing. As new discoveries are made in science and medicine, forensic psychologists must apply them to their practices. For example, many new drugs are introduced each year to treat medical conditions. Some drugs are just for people who suffer from **insomnia**. As more people take these drugs, the behavioral side effects become more apparent.

Sometimes, people taking certain sleeping pills discover they have done strange things in their sleep. They ate cake mix in bed. They did repair work on their

20

Each person reacts a little differently to sleeping pills.

homes. They even drove their cars. And they don't remember any of it! Good forensic psychologists must keep up with such information. They might have to interview a driver in a hit-and-run case to see if such medications were involved.

Bullying is a subject that many people are concerned with today. People are becoming more aware of children and adults who have "snapped" after being bullied extensively. They suddenly commit violent acts that seem out of character. Psychologists are now identifying

Many soldiers have PTSD when they return home from war.

specific behaviors of bullies and the people who are their victims. For meaningful interviews, forensic psychologists need to understand how both types of people think and act.

Another issue that forensic psychologists are studying is post-**traumatic** stress disorder, or PTSD. This disorder affects some people who have lived through a terrible ordeal. A teen who was seriously injured in a car accident, a child who lived through a tornado, or a young man returning from battle might all show signs of PTSD. People with this disorder react in abnormal or extreme ways to stressful situations. Forensic psychologists are keeping up with the latest discoveries about PTSD. Their information might help them determine which parent might be the better caregiver for a traumatized child. It might help them spot a security guard applicant who would respond inappropriately to a dangerous situation.

THINK ABOUT SCIENCE

Researchers say that PTSD stems from memories of very scary events. But how do these memories form? Certain chemicals in the brain help us to form them. Geneticists, biochemists, and neuroscientists are trying to understand the details. Forensic psychologists, meanwhile, are keeping up with their discoveries. Every little bit of information helps them understand people with PTSD.

CHAPTER 5

Becoming a Forensic Psychologist

If you are considering forensic psychology as a career, you will need both education and experience. But the best forensic psychologists have certain personal qualities, too. They are patient and have a real desire to help others. They withhold judgments and try to understand people and their motivations. They are comfortable working with many different kinds of individuals.

Most forensic psychologists start by earning a bachelor's degree. This usually takes four years of college. Psychology is a good choice for a major. But statistics, life sciences, or sociology would be good majors, too, if they included psychology classes. With a bachelor's degree, a graduate might be able to work as a parole or probation officer or assist at a counseling center.

Some forensic psychologists work in prisons as counselors.

A master's degree in psychology or forensic psychology usually takes two or three years more. In these classes, students often do their own research and learn how the legal system works. A graduate might work as a psychologist in a prison, juvenile facility, hospital, or addiction treatment center. He or she might also assist a researcher or a working forensic psychologist who has a doctoral degree.

The doctoral degree requires about three more years of study. This program calls for further coursework, research, and work with patients. Graduates must pass an exam to receive a license to practice psychology. At this point, the forensic psychologist may work in a psychiatric hospital, teach at a university, open a private office, or work for the court system or the Federal Bureau of Investigation (FBI). A forensic psychologist at this level makes around $75,000 to $120,000 annually.

Some forensic psychologists work in hospitals.

At one time, psychology had little influence in the legal system. Today, we realize that human behavior is complex. To deal with legal and human issues fairly, we need sensitivity and scientific insight. Forensic psychologists are the ideal people to work within this fascinating field.

THINK ABOUT ART

Of course, forensic psychologists should understand psychology and the law. But they must also be good writers. They should be able to summarize an interview or an impression in sharp, clear language. They must choose words and phrases that convey exactly what they want to say. For this reason, many forensic psychologists have taken writing classes in college.

A forensic psychologist can have a strong impact on the outcome of a trial.

THINK ABOUT IT

Forensic psychologists often must interview young children. What are some personality traits they need in order to do this job well?

Today, some forensic psychologists are learning about differences between people from different cultures. Why would this be important to their work?

Some researchers are studying how violent video games affect the behavior of the games' players. Do you think it's important to look into this? Why or why not?

After reading this book, do you think that forensic psychologists might actually save people's lives? If so, how?

LEARN MORE

FURTHER READING

Kincher, Jonni. *Psychology for Kids Vol. 2: 40 Fun Experiments That Help You Learn About Others.* Minneapolis: Free Spirit Publishing, 2008.

Shone, Rob. *Solving Crimes Through Criminal Profiling.* New York: Rosen Publishing Group, 2008.

Williams, Judith. *Forensic Scientist: Careers Solving Crimes and Scientific Mysteries.* New York: Enslow Publishing, 2009.

WEB SITES

American Board of Forensic Psychology
www.abfp.com/brochure.asp
Learn more about what forensic psychologists do.

Psychology Today: What's It Take to Become a Forensic Psychologist?
www.psychologytoday.com/blog/witness/201010/whats-it-take-become-forensic
-psychologist
Learn about the skills and training needed to become a forensic psychologist.

GLOSSARY

arson (AHR-suhn) the crime of setting fire to property with the intention of destroying it

custody (KUHS-tuh-dee) the legal right to care for a child

defendant (di-FEN-duhnt) someone who is accused of a crime

exaggerating (ig-ZAJ-uh-rate-eng) magnifying a story beyond what is truthful

expertise (ek-spur-TEEZ) special skill or knowledge

expert witness (EK-spurt WIT-nis) someone with special knowledge or skills who testifies at trials

eyewitness (eye-WIT-nis) a person who claims to have seen a crime or event take place

forensic (for-EN-sik) pertaining to a court of law

incarcerated (in-KAR-sur-ay-ted) placed in prison or in confinement

insight (IN-site) the ability to understand something that is not obvious

insomnia (in-SOM-nee-uh) an inability to fall or stay asleep

legitimate (luh-JIT-uh-mit) in accordance with the law or with normal rules or standards

traumatic (traw-MAT-ik) relating to a serious wound, shock, or injury

witnesses (WIT-nis-ez) people who testify and give evidence at a trial

INDEX

[21ST CENTURY SKILLS LIBRARY]